A
MOTHER'S
TONGUE

Carolyn Denise

Jawbone
PUBLISHING CORPORATION

www.JawbonePublishing.com

published by Jawbone Publishing corporation
2907 PAddington Way
Kissimmee, Florida 34747
www.JawbonePublishing.com

printed in the United States of America

ISBN 1-59094-058X

Table of Contents

Dedication

This book is dedicated to my mother, Agnes Bass; to my God-parents, Mr. Henry and Mrs. Louise McDaniel; and to all thirteen of my sisters and brothers – Angela, Cynthia, Willie, Thelma, Yvette, Charles, Richard, Robert, Hank, Terry, Stephen, Chris, and Henry, Jr. (I love you guys and could not be where I am today without the support of my large and wonderful family. May each of you continue to grow in Jesus.); to our children, grandchildren, nieces, and nephews and to all of the boys and girls I have had the pleasure of teaching over the last five years. Your parents, without thinking sometimes release harsh words. When that happens, you may feel extremely hurt by the words released. Please find the grace in your heart to forgive them. Be determined not to repeat the cycle, and remember, above all else, choose to love.

Foreword

Carolyn Denise Kemp is a woman of God who has trusted God, no matter what she has come up against. The trials and test that she has overcome is a testimony to many. By watching her, they are assured of their victory in Christ.

Carolyn is a woman of faith, and we know God always honors those who trust in Him, which explains why Carolyn is so blessed. Carolyn is now soaring in the blessings of God. God spoke it, and she believed it. Soar like an eagle, Carolyn Denise Kemp.

Mrs. Willie Coller

On a personal note

My Sister,

You are a women who has stood on God's word and, no matter what it looked or sounded like, you trusted God and believed in His word. Carolyn, you have been an example of faith and love; you have practiced the meaning of love within the family, through the good and bad times. I believe that the best is yet to come for you. God is about to reward you with such a magnitude of His power, because of your faithfulness.

I love you, Sis. I believe in you and the Christ you serve. Continue demonstrating God's glory in your life.

Love, your sister,

Mrs. Willie Coller

Introduction

Why is this book needed?

Because ...

If a boy believes he's a failure,

then he is.

If a girl believes she's a failure,

then she is.

If a boy believes he's a success,

then he is.

If a girl believes she's a success,

then she is.

Question is,

What do you believe about you?

And what will

your children believe

about themselves

after you have raised them?

Chapter One

Why This Book is Needed

What is it you believe that has so shaped your mindset and your worldview? Is your worldview shaped by God and the principles in the Bible or by this naturalistic world? Do you believe we are the result of a transcendent God, or are we the result of nature doing its thing? These questions are crucial, because one behaves in the manner he thinks.

Your speaking, action, and decision-making will all be a result of your thinking process. If you believe in the one and only true living God, the Creator of the heaven and the earth, Jehovah, the first and the last, then you should also believe in His principles and live them daily. Believing is not enough.

This book is written because even as a Christian educator working with Christian parents daily, I see the results of people who believe, yet are not walking in that belief. I see its evidence, sadly to say, in our children. Children are suffering daily at the lips of abusers; but because there are no outward scars, the problem is overlooked.

I have dealt with children in all categories listed in this book concerning verbal abuse. Verbal abuse is not limited to calling a child out of their name, as you will read later. There are other forms — and oh, how subtle it can be. I am sure some parents are operating out of pure ignorance. They are only repeating a cycle that for generations has been the way their family has done things.

Then there are those abusers who are cunning, callous, and know exactly what wicked goal they are trying to accomplish with each word released. Are they aiming for bitterness, low-self esteem, doubt, fear or control? Only God knows.

I find these types of verbal abusers to be in the same category as pedophiles. One who is, with all understanding, purposely setting out to destroy a child. A child, mind you, one of God's most precious creations. The defenseless emotions and spirit of a child fall prey to these abusers.

Why? Because of power and control. Satan wanted it in heaven. We all know someone who wants it in the work place or in our churches. From the beginning, we have been trying to have rule and power over one another. Yet God constantly admonishes us to love, submit, and humble ourselves before one another.

God advises us to not provoke our children, but to love and care for them. The fact that God tells us to spank them, yet never tells us to scream/yell/or call them out of their names, should be some indication that verbal abuse is much more harmful to a child then a paddle on the bottom. Remember, God is always right.

This society and its naturalistic worldview is ready to lock a mother up for spanking her child. They, on the other hand, let a man who calls his three year old daughter a" good for nothing whore" walk freely amongst us saying, "He did no wrong." Yet when this child turns 16 and begins to live the prophecy of her father, we call her a bad kid. I beg to differ!

This book, simply to say, is written because my God had something to say and He used me to say it. He loves our children and would like to share with us the damage we do when we release negative words into their lives. The hurt they feel when we call them out of their names.

Please be wise enough to receive this message from God. And if you are guilty of this kind of abuse, repent quickly. If you hear parents verbally abusing their children, give them a copy of this book.

With God, our mercies are new every morning, so we have the opportunity to repent and start over.

Make an appointment with your child. Apologize to him. Assure him that, from now on, things are going to be different. Walk in love. Walk in grace. Walk in Jesus.

In short, this book is written to off set verbal abuse. To expose the evil and its attack on our children by their very own mothers and other family members. It is titled *A Mother's Tongue* because usually with children, no tongue matters like that of their mothers.

A mother can make or break a child, just by wagging her tongue. We must remember as mothers that every inch of us belongs to God, and we are to honor Him with the words that are released from our mouths and onto our children. *A Mother's Tongue* is written to help us recognize and defuse negative speaking. This knowledge gives us an opportunity to change and move on. We can change our lives, effectively change an entire generation … so on and so forth, by making positive choices about the words we are about to release.

Grab hold of the power of positive words

and use them

to express yourself

and your child's greatness.

Love 'ya!

Chapter Two

Leroy Brown

Follow me for a while as I travel down this path of understanding

- why our children behave as they do.

- why we have immature adults still living at home, drinking milk from a bottle, and crying every time they hear the word *no*. (While, on the other hand we have productive citizens who are out of the house and school, and who are living an abundantly productive life.)

Before we start our traveling adventure, let me assure you that I **don't** believe every situation is the same. I understand that some mothers have spoken nothing but life and health into their children's lives, and yet some children have chosen a life of destruction. Other mothers have spoken nothing but death, but by the grace of God those children made it through victoriously. We will review a couple of cases in point and reveal the defeats and victories that can happen because of a *Mother's Tongue*.

Are you ready? Will you follow me on this journey? Maybe you will find yourself in some of the characters mentioned in this book. Let's go!

Travel with me as I review the lives of a few special people who have helped so many. Our journey begins with Leroy Brown ...

Let us first look at the case with Leroy. Leroy is now 42 and living at home with his mother.

What happened, why is he back home? Where did things go wrong?

Let's go back. Back to the home where this baby ran around and played. Enter the room this young person called home. Let's travel to the crib where this toddler slept peacefully. To the arms that brought this infant home. To the Mother … yes, go back to the mother.

"It's a boy!" Doctor Ross proclaimed. "You are the proud parent of a baby boy. What are you going to name him?" she asked.

"Leroy. His name is Leroy David Brown."

"That's a good name," the doctor said. "He'll grow up to be a very important man some day."

"I hope so," replied the mother.

While holding little Leroy in her arms, she added, "I hope he isn't anything like his old no-good daddy."

Bam! There we have it. Leroy is officially 5 minutes old and already hit with the negativity of his *Mother's Tongue*.

Leroy is the youngest of three children. The other two children have their own daddy and Leroy has his.

The first daddy visits, buys for, and takes very good care of his children. Leroy has never seen his daddy.

Leroy's mother is very hurt and disgusted by her baby's daddy, yet not surprised by his behavior. You see, Leroy's daddy has four other children, all living with their own mommas. Leroy's momma was promised love, marriage, and security. He even treated her other children, girls, like his own.

But things turned sour when momma found out Leroy was on the way. Daddy didn't want any other kids. He felt tricked, trapped. So, he ran.

The family, then, consists of Leroy, his two sisters, and momma. Leroy is the brunt of all his sisters' jokes, and his mother's anger. "Our Daddy loves us. You don't even know who your daddy is," they would ridicule.

"I could be living high off the hog if it wasn't for you," his mother would blurt out. "I should have had an abortion," she told him on numerous occasions.

Leroy withdrew into himself with each and every negative retort.

Leroy is now ten years old. He has taken a turn for the worst. He has had enough. Someone called him a four-eyed freak, and he snapped. Leroy has decided to take matters into his own hands.

Is it possible that Leroy is now becoming the person his mother and sisters have called him for the past 10 years? Is it true that he is just like his daddy? Or has his mother's tongue shaped his life?

Leroy never knew his daddy, so the only information he has received was from his mother's tongue. And that was extremely negative.

Leroy, now 13, has been kicked out of school for the third time. He is no longer allowed on the school bus.

"What am I going to do with you Leroy?"

"You get on my nerves; I have tried everything with you."

"Are you just stupid, boy?"

"Do you want to end up in jail?"

"Why can't you behave like your sisters?"

"They don't give me a lick of trouble."

Let us examine why.

Chapter Three

The Examination of Leroy Brown

Since his birth, Leroy has been told he was not wanted, useless and a good-for-nothing. His sisters have been hearing the "we wanted you and we love you" tape all of their lives, while Leroy has really been raised an *orphan*. He lives in a house where he is unwanted and has been given minimal care. His basic needs of food and shelter needs have been met. However, if he wanted a hug, he was pushed away while the girls were embraced. He was never encouraged when he made a "B" ... unless "it's about time" is considered an encouraging phrase.

Yes, Leroy has been thrown into a well of destruction. Each disparaging word lowers him deeper and deeper into the well.

We as a society have to start recognizing and dealing with verbal abuse. Verbal abuse, HEAR THIS LOUD AND CLEAR, is a silent killer.

And

The Cycle

Continues.

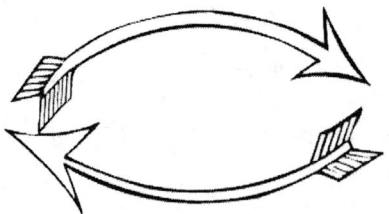

Now 19, Leroy is about to become a father. Deciding he doesn't want his child to grow up unwanted and without a dad, Leroy marries. He brings into the marriage all of the baggage from his past.

His new wife has no idea what she is marrying into, because Leroy has been on his own since he was 17. She has never met his family.

On his twentieth birthday, Leroy becomes a daddy. He is overwhelmed with emotions and begins to cry — something he hasn't done in at least ten years.

As the new couple and baby begin to live their lives, the past raises its ugly, unhealed head. Leroy believes that just because he stays, he is a better man than his dad was. But what Leroy does not understand is that he has brought with him all of the verbal abuse he has learned from his mom.

After five years, Leroy leaves.

Leroy has now fathered five children through four mommas.

What had Leroy done?

Let's journey on a side road back home to momma. Let's go back to that comment five minutes after his birth. Had Leroy given any indication that he was going to be a no-good bum, leaving babies all over Chicago? As he got older, was it his fault that the girl's daddy took care of them and his daddy didn't?

Yet, Leroy was ridiculed from birth because of the choices his mother made. She decided to have unprotected sex with a man with a reputation. Was she speaking out of her own hurt each time she ripped a pound of flesh from that baby's soul? Was it her own shame, embarrassment, and lack of judgment she saw each time that he reached for a hug?

Whatever the cause, her tongue caused great damage to this young man's spirit. He begins to fulfill her prophecy and act like his father. Mind you, the only knowledge of this man came from her mouth. What if her mental "it"(studied in my book, *Cause I'm a Woman*) wasn't so damaged?

Oh, how things could have turned out differently. What if she had said, "Leroy, you are a genius, just like your daddy? I am so proud of you. I know your daddy isn't a part of your life, but, hey, I got you babe! It's me and you, kid, all the way."

Even if getting pregnant with Leroy was an accident, was it necessary to tell him?

Her tongue could have made all the difference in the world.

As mothers, our children listen to us, even when we think they are not listening. My oldest confessed to me, "Mom, I am listening, even if I act like I'm not."

A few years later, my youngest made the same statement.

Both in their own time zoned revealed that when they are out with their friends, a lot of what I say to them comes out. Their dad and I are not together, yet I make it a point to tell them how smart he was in school and how much he loves them. They love the story of how he acted when we found out each of them were on the way.

My children know they are here with purpose, and so does each child in my classroom. I tell them weekly, "God wanted you here, and you are of great value. You bring God great joy."

What if we, as mothers, use our tongues to speak the truth of God's word? What if we make a stand to determine in our hearts and families that we will no longer use our tongues to breed damaged Leroy's, but healed healthy positive ones?

What if!

There are many Leroys in this world. Children who were unwanted at birth; children who have lived with that reality for many years.

I am one of those children. I was told that repeatedly throughout my childhood. But I know God wanted and does want us. He died, so that we might live. If you are a mother who has spoken words of harm, it is not too late to reverse the damage of your tongue and begin to speak life into your child.

Your son does not have to repeat the mistakes of his father. He can have a new start through Jesus. If you know your tongue has been the weapon used to beat your child down, begin to pray and read the Bible. Ask God for wisdom and direction on how your tongue can now be used as part of the healing process.

No matter how bad the situation, it doesn't have to end in the red. God is a redeemer of the negative tongues and the Leroys who are damaged by them. I am a product of such redemption, and so is this book. Give God an opportunity to prove Himself faithful to you, as well.

Be healed by the spoken words

released from His tongue

to man's ears,

minds,

and hearts.

Leroy has come full circle. He is back home with momma. Momma, who has since given her life to Jesus, realizes all of the things she has done wrong concerning her son. She is extremely apologetic for the words she used against him, for the names she called him, and for telling him several times he was unwanted. She now understands that God, according to Psalm 139, knew all about Leroy and was excited about his arrival. She tries to share with Leroy her Jesus and the plan of salvation, but Leroy is not interested.

As they continue to live together, they both begin to notice things about each other and themselves. Leroy notices that his sisters rarely call, and that his mother has not said one negative thing about them or their lack of concern for her. He sees her reading her Bible daily and begins to wonder if there really is something to this Christ stuff.

He so longs to have healing and peace from the negative tapes in his mind. He also notices that even though she was abusively hard on him as a child, he loves her.

Mom notices that the girls don't call often and they do not visit. They are ashamed of her poverty and their brother. She has offered them Jesus, but they don't have time for that religious stuff. She also notices that the man she despised as a child is the one who is actually taking care of her in her old age.

She cries out to God for forgiveness. She prays for hours apologizing for every hurt, pain, and negative word that she had said or done to Leroy.

Leroy is standing outside of his mother's door. He hears her prayer and is convinced that she is sorry and that there is a God. He forgives his mother, accepts the God of the Bible, and spends the rest of his life taking care of his mother and being a Godly father to his children.

Your story may not end like this one. Your mother may never get saved, never apologize, or even want you in her life. But none of those things can stop you from being healed from the verbal abuse.

Make a choice to accept healing and forgive your mother, even if she never asks you for forgiveness. Healing is a choice; choose it.

You're grown now. Put away childhood hurts through the blood of Jesus, and vow never to be a culprit by which verbal abuse is allowed to live and breathe.

Oh, Lord, You have searched me and know me. You know my sitting down and my rising up. You understand my thoughts from afar — even before I think them. You are acquainted with all my ways; there is not a word on my tongue, Lord, that you don't know.

You have laid Your hand on me. Where can I go from Your presence or where can I flee from Your spirit? If I ascend into heaven, You are there. If I make my bed in hell, even there You shall find me.

I am no accident to you. You knew all about me before my mother found out I was coming. You are the one who knitted me together and placed me in my mother's womb. You chose my eyes, hair, cheeks and heart; You fearfully and wonderfully put me together and then placed me in my mother's womb.

You have nothing but wonderful thoughts about me. You think I am great. You love me with a love that is immeasurable.

Never will I again allow the words of others to hinder my growth and service for you.

Nor will I allow my tongue to render or release words of destruction on Your other fearfully and wonderfully created vessels.

Proverbs 18:21 — Death and life are in the power of the tongue and they that love it shall eat the fruit thereof. (KJV)

1 Peter 3:10 — For he that love life and see good days let him refrain his tongue from evil, and speak no guile.

John 16:1 — These things have I spoken unto you, that ye should not be offended (Greek- *skandalidzo*: meaning to stumble to fall to distrust, and desert one, in which he ought trust and obey)

Our tongues

should not be used

to tear down

but to build up.

Chapter Four

Sherry

This next form of verbal abuse is more personal; I have actually lived and walked through this pain. Unlike Leroy's attacks on his lineage, this abuse attacks the person due to outward appearance.

We see this daily at work, school and play. A person looks different from the so-called norm. So hey, they are open for personal ridicule.

Again, as you will learn from a child's view, no one's tongue really mattered like their mother's tongue.

What did Sherry's mother's tongue tell her?

"You are so fat. No man is ever going to marry you. You are going to be stuck at home with a bunch of kids and on welfare."

Wow! Ouch. What was wrong with that mother's tongue?

All her life obesity was a problem for Sherry. But as a child, she never knew it was a problem. Not until her mother's negative, abusive tongue went into action.

Sherry ran and played with the boys. She climbed trees, caught grasshoppers, played on the railroad tracks, and could still out-jump any girl in double Dutch. She was the fastest runner on the thirteenth floor. So, exactly what was the problem, with Sherry?

Absolutely nothing. The problem was with Sherry's mother. Sherry was more robust than the other girls and boys her age. So to her unhealthy mom, Sherry was open to ridicule.

Sherry was dragged around from one weight loss clinic to the next. She was ridiculed, talked about, and denied privileges until she lost weight. Sherry noticed that when she would lose weight, approval and acceptance was abundant. But when she gained weight, verbal abuse was just as abundant. So Sherry sought approval from her unhealthy mother. (My book, *'Cause I'm a Woman*, delves at length into our unhealthy "it".)

Sherry soon found herself seeking her mom's approval in other areas, as well as eating. But nothing worked. Just like a diet, she had quick gratification and then greater failure than before.

Sherry began to wet the bed. This only added to her shame, as she would come home from school and find her mattress airing outside. Beatings and verbal abuse followed the bed wetting, followed by overeating and weight gain.

We must realize, as parents, that we cannot shame our children into the behavioral change we are seeking.

Verbal abuse is one form of abuse that has gone on far too long without comprehension of the damage it causes. Many people brag that they have never hit their children, only to realize that when an attack with negative words is, in fact, hitting them. Verbal abuse hurts worse than any belt ever could.

The scars from my physical beatings are long gone. But the scars from my verbal beatings are still present today. My warning to mothers and mothers-to-be about the words we speak onto your children comes from personal experience. Experience that, as a parent, I am not proud of. I still see the results of some of my negative tongue. Experience from my childhood as a recipient of such abuse.

We can say until the cats come home and the dogs begin to meow that we are not going to hurt our children, as we were hurt. But until we get healed ourselves, the likelihood of the negative behavior repeating itself is great.

I got help. I read books. And I prayed, prayed, and prayed again.

Lord, I remember what it felt like to be hollered at

I don't want my kids to feel like that.

In my heart, I love them more than words can say.

Help me to show them how much I love and care for them.

Help me, Lord, to break the cycle of negativity in our family.

May I love them as You love me.

Teach me, Lord, when to spank, when to talk,

and when it just doesn't matter.

Help me not to make a deal out of nothing,

and to understand when the boys are just being kids.

Lord, please give me the wisdom I need

to raise these boys for Your glory.

I have never been a parent before,

and I don't like some of the things I am doing.

Please help me.

God did, indeed, answer my prayer. He has and is helping me raise my sons for His glory.

I have felt the blow of verbal abuse and dealt it. It doesn't feel good, no matter which end you are on. I can only imagine it being worse for children, because they feel so powerless.

As we all know, power is usually the root to most forms of abuse. The abuser wants to feel powerful over the abused. Why else would a grown man snatch a nine-year-old from a bed and violate her, when he could buy sex for ten dollars? Because violating that baby makes him feel powerful.

Maybe somewhere along his journey, he was fed by a negative tongue. And now he needs to feel in charge and powerful; so he uses sex to regain the power that he feels was stripped from him. He, like his abuser, violates someone unable to fight back.

Verbal abuse strips a person of self-worth. It also makes one feel useless, defeated, and powerless. Usually when people grow up with such negativity, they transfer that trait to the next generation, (in psychology, it is called "Split-Trait") and so on and so forth, until the cycle is broken by the word of God.

The tongue is a two-edged sword. We use it to curse and to bless ... to edify and to bring down. The Bible asks, "Does both sweet and bitter water come from the same faucet?"

Neither should we speak both curses and blessings to our children. We need to remember at all times, regardless of how our children were conceived; they are a blessing (gift) from Him. Our tongues can lead them into their destiny or into danger.

Most children are seeking from us the same thing we are seeking from God. Acceptance. God has, in His wisdom, made it abundantly clear that we were totally accepted before we lived out one day. Before the doctor ever told our parents we were on the way. Should we do any less for our children?

Should we make them feel unwanted, useless, a-good-for-nothing, because they are chubby, skinny, wears glasses, light, dark, bucktooth, cross-eyed, short, tall, talk with a slur, or stutters? Did our children select any of these traits for themselves?

The children had nothing to do with their outward shells and should never be talked down to, especially about any of their outward features. If they act like daddy, remember who picked daddy. You. Not them.

If there are negative traits, work on them as you accentuate the positive traits about your child. A mother's tongue is a very powerful weapon. This one weapon alone can cause great success or failure. Most children wait for what momma has to say over all others.

Children yearn to hear something wonderful about themselves as they prepare to leave for the prom. You blurt out, "I bet you wish you would have lost that twenty pounds now, don't you?"

Your son comes home and announces, "Mom, it has been six months and I have not had a car accident!"

You respond, "It's about time."

We have all heard — if not spoken them ourselves — the following phrases: "You're so stupid", or "That was dumb," or "You are just so sorry, you pig," and "No one will marry you," and the list goes on.

There is something

Each and every one of us

Can do.

Help is available.

God is able

To control the tongue.

You can speak life!

Let us all SHUT OUT verbal abuse!

May we settle in our hearts

that we are going to be positive…

that we will edify our children

and not tear them down

with the words of our tongues.

Let us make it abundantly clear

to our children

that though the world

may be speaking against them,

they have an advocate in us.

May the phrase, "I'm in your corner, kid"

be an ever present thought

of our love for them.

Learn to apologize.

Now that we know better, we must do better. A true sign of our healing is the willingness to apologize to our children and to God.

Apologize to your kids and to God for past behavior. Pick up a new way of loving your kids. Love them in words and deeds (actions). Make a vow to yourself, to God, and to a friend, that you will never cause your child to lower his head in shame because of a series of negative words released by your tongue.

The Creator did not give you that tongue for the purpose of abuse. Especially when the receiver of the abuse is one of His most defenseless creations.

Time does not heal all wounds.

A simple apology can

heal hurts and save time.

Today no matter your children's ages, connect with them somehow and let them know you love them and accept them with no strings attached.

Just the way they are.

Love produces the positive results we desire. Ridicule and/or shame will not.

What happened to Sherry? She grew up to be a very beautiful, educated woman. But she never believed it. Instead, she continued to believe her mother's negative tongue.

"You are going to be fat all of your life."

"No one will ever want you because you are fat."

No matter what Sherry accomplished, she felt like a failure because of her waistline. Sherry tried every diet on the market. She even tried some illegal ones. If there was an ad about losing weight, she tried it, only to feel more and more like a failure with each disappointing failed attempt at losing weight.

Sherry moved away from home. Every now and then, she would visit her mother only to find out things had not changed. Her mother's tongue was still a whip that attacked Sherry on every hand.

"You're still fat," she would say. "You have a cute face."

Sherry received that remark as if to say, "The rest of you isn't worth mentioning."

Never mind that Sherry had a successful career, marriage, and was financially independent — things that her mother had never obtained. Sherry could never gain her mother's approval. Her mother's tongue never stopped. She constantly released negative comments about Sherry's weight.

Sherry found some of her childhood pictures and realized that she wasn't an obese child, after all. But it was too late; the damage had been done. Sherry had accepted the years of negativity about her weight, so in her mind, she believed she was fat.

Over the years, she lived up to her mother's prophecy and began to get larger and larger. With each gained pound, she hated herself and her mother more and more.

Sherry had her stomached stapled and later died of complications. Not yet forty years old, she was gone. The world lost a beautiful woman, a family lost a mother, and I lost a friend.

A mother's tongue carries great weight. Our children only want our acceptance. They are screaming for us to love them just the way that they are. Yet we ridicule and reject them over things of such little importance.

Make the time to assure your children, regardless of their ages, of their value to you.

My children know that they know I love them. I know they love me. When we have to deal with difficult situations (and you all will), I make it a point to deal with the issue and not attack them personally.

God never attacks us; He always attacks the sin.

Sherry's mom could have saved her daughter's life by just accepting her as a little girl. Everyone else did. Sherry never cared about all of the other tongues that wagged at her. There was only one tongue from which she wanted to hear, "I love you and accept you." Her mother's tongue.

Sadly, Sherry never heard those three special words. She only read them at the end of a letter after she had left home for good.

May the words of this book prevent more tragedies such as Sherry's, Leroy's Carolyn's Suzanne's and _____ (You fill in the blank. Maybe it will be your name on the dotted line. Most of us have been there in one form or another, so it just as well is your name on the blank. But, praise God, if you follow the principles in this book, it will never have to be your child's name.)

Make a difference in your family. Stop verbal abuse. If you hear it in your family, give the abuser a copy of this book. Stand up to the abuser and make the person aware of what is being done. Encourage children to talk about things that were said to them.

Words that hurt or hinder cause shame and tears. Let the children know how valuable they are and that it is the adult with the problem, not them.

We want to kill people who abuse children sexually, yet we

see verbal abuse as no big deal. Well, it is a big deal. Anything
that is spoken and causes a level of death in our children's spirit is
a big deal.

Once in a parking lot, I heard a father just ripping his three-
year-old apart with his tongue. I mean, he was just letting her
have it. He used words that pimps and whores use with each
other — not fathers and daughters.

I said to him, "It doesn't take all of that."

He just looked as if to say, "Mind your own business."

I wrote down his license plate number and called the child
abuse hot line. I told them everything that had happened. The
counselor told me that was not abuse, and that they couldn't send
a child advocate out, based on verbal abuse.

I assured him that it is a form of abuse and we, as a society,
need to start recognizing it. Most of the High school shootings are
a result of children that had been ridiculed and taunted. Maxed
out, they decided to regain some control by shooting fellow
classmates. They tried to prove to themselves and classmates that
they really weren't the dorks people claim them to be. **Word's
hurt!**

Good people are lost daily or are wasting away by the side of the road. Some are drowning themselves in a bottle, while others are pumping drugs into their veins. Then we have those who are hiding behind the snack cake (like I once did), career, husband, children, anything that they can hide in, on, or under. Why? Because they are not willing to, ready to, or capable of dealing with the words that taunt their minds day in and day out.

The words that were released by someone's tongue.

Each of us must look at ourselves first. What have I done to help or hinder a person's life? What criticism and/or sarcastic remarks am I releasing in the name of fun or joking, not realizing real damage is taking place? How can I help stamp out verbal abuse? Where do I start?

We start in our hearts as a commitment to change and do better. Then we branch out to those in our homes. Rather than our friends, we would start in our households, with our spouses and children. Make it a point that everyone in your home is loved by you, valued by you, and special to you.

My nephew, Terry, visits weekly, sometimes a few days, sometimes a week or so. He lives up the street and around the corner, so home is not far away. He loves coming over here. He knows, without a doubt, I love him like my own two sons.

He never feels second to them. He jumps in my bed to watch TV quicker then my two would. He knows where everything is. I give him chores, and reading assignments like I give my own sons.

The point is, no matter who is in your home, make an effort to assure them of their value.

If you find it difficult to praise people, it is because you are still being healed yourself. Just think of how Jesus feels about them. He thought they were worth dying for. Why should you think anything less?

Chapter Five

Interjection

I want to interject something at this point. I don't want any of the readers to be left with the message, "I am the way I am because, so I guess I'll just stay here."

I strongly believe that, as children in the hands of an abuser, we may feel hopeless, intimidated, and very frightened. As children, we may not know the who, what, where, or how to get help.

But as adults, we need to get up, get help and get moving.

That was the difference between Sherry and me. We both had weight problems; we both suffered verbal abuse because of it. We both had a negative "mother's tongue" in our lives. But Sherry still needed her mother's approval, while I decided I didn't. Sherry tried one more thing to get approval.

I wrote a long letter to my mother and said good-bye. I told her of all the things she had said that hurt me. I told her how she made me feel about my weight. And some of the other things that were done that hurt me. I wrote, "I am writing this letter with the understanding that I may be kicked out of the family. But in order to be healed emotionally, I am willing to take that chance."

Everyone rejected me, except my oldest sister. She stated, "Everyone doesn't have your courage, Carolyn."

I am sure I will be frowned on again for having this section in the book. My job is to obey Christ and help set the captives free. Verbal abuse has run too long and too deep in all of our families. People are wasting away because they believe they are a good-for-nothing.

God Himself is screaming, **"Hey, don't listen to them. I think you are great, valuable. See, I even sent my son to die, so that you could join me here in heaven. C'mon, lift up your hung-down head. You are worth something to me."**

Oh, how I wish Sherry could have received that message. I would still have her here with me today. She would never believe she was beautiful and talented, just the way she was. She so needed the approval of outside forces.

The weight did not make or break her. But the words she remembered hearing as a child taunted her.

We both would relate each of our failures back to our childhood words.

You may say, "Carolyn, I am not as strong as you are. I can't take the chance of losing my family. I am more like Sherry; I would rather conform to others expected end."

I say, there will never be an end. As an adult, once you start conforming to someone's negative tongue, it never ends.

Abuse, regardless of the form in which it appears, is usually about control. God never intended for us to release control of our lives to anyone. He gave it to us to live and live it in abundance and great joy.

You can get up off the side of the road, off the depression medicine, out of the person's house, if you're still there, and move! Get off the couch, out of the bed, out of the dead end job where you are just hiding away from the world. Begin to live the new, true message about you!

The strangest thing happened after I made my move towards healing. Unlike Sherry, I didn't die. I began to live. Within six months, I was able to look into the mirror and tell myself I was pretty, in spite of my size. I was able to say, "I love you, and really mean it."

I started having good thoughts about myself. My mom and I did not speak for almost three years. But I was on the road to recovery, and I was staying there.

Now I think about *me* everything God thinks about me. I can say with ease that I love me — every one of these 199 pounds of me. I stand in the mirror singing, "I'm too sexy for myself" song. I walk like I love me. I talk like I love me. I treat me like I love me. Because I do love me.

The little girls in the classroom decided to imitate my walk, and, boy, were they doing a good job. They tell me I walk real *girly*. I get an opportunity five days a week to impart Godly principles and positive words into their precious little spirits daily.

In my classroom, you won't hear children crying because someone was talking about them. My students will tell you quick, fast and in a hurry, "God has more good thoughts about me than there are grains of sand. I believe God, not you."

One co-worker told me I walk around with my head up in the air like I don't need anyone. I assured her that God made us to need each other, but that my head being up was part of my healing … that for years I wasn't able to look in the mirror and say I was pretty. I assured her that I was not stuck up; I was healed.

I am determined not to allow anyone to knock me off the healthy road. She confessed to me that, to this day, she is unable to look in the mirror and say she is or feels pretty. Thing is, she is smaller than I am. So again, we see that weight really isn't the issue.

The issue is what words have been released into you and why as an adult you are still believing them.

All around us are damaged people, and misery loves company. The co-worker was just jealous because I was able to walk in what she was so longing and needing; acceptance of God just the way she is.

Damaged people are everywhere. They are damaged by the silent killer, *verbal abuse* and they want you to join them. *Verbal Abuse* is a silent killer we can all destroy, just by submitting the words we release out of our months to God first.

Always consider the other person's feelings. Who will be receiving the words we are about to release today?

My change started with me getting up, making a move, and trusting God. You too can do this, so let's go! Forget about the past, grab hold of the healer and be healed.

NO MORE EXCUSES,

You're grown now. No one can hurt you, unless you allow it. You don't have to die; you can live. God is able to teach you all of the wonderful things about *you* that make you so special.

Chapter Six

Sherry Continues

Both Sherry and I had people speaking positive, wonderful things into our lives. But we just couldn't see it. My sister, Willie, would always tell me I was sexy and that I have beautiful eyes. I can see now that I do have beautiful eyes. And there is nothing wrong with a Christian woman feeling and looking good about herself. Feeling good about yourself as a woman tends to make you feel sexy. (Don't be afraid to say *Christian woman* and *sexy* in the same sentence. Everything I have God gave to me; I honor Him with this body.)

I am also mindful of the believer who thinks being covered from head to toe is the way to go. Pray about everything. God has promised to lead us if we acknowledge Him in our situations.

The Bible assures us that God has more good thoughts about us than there are grains of sand. So, why not have a few good thoughts about yourself?

Enough time has been wasted thinking about the lies spoken

to us as children. Don't allow anyone or anything to place you back into bondage. God set you free, remain free. Freedom is worth fighting for.

Throughout history, freedom was sought after, fought for, and attained. Don't back out now. Promise yourself that the only words that will ever move you again emotionally are the words of God.

His words are true pure and honest. His words have no secret jealous, envious motive. His words breathe life, my friends, so inhale the life of God and live.

Choose life and live!

Negative words hurt.

Negative words hurt.

Negative words hurt.

Negative words hurt.

Negative words hurt.

Negative words hurt.

Negative words hurt.

Negative words hurt.

Be a part of the solution.

Speak positive words!

Chapter Seven

Suzanne

Verbal abuse is evident in several forms:

- talking down to your children because of their outward features
- speaking negatively to them because of their heritage.

Verbal abuse hurts and it kills.

End it today.

Another form of verbal abuse is speaking against your children because of their lack of academic abilities. This form of abuse is seen on television often and laughed at regularly.

Verbal abuse is the releasing of words that causes a person to feel belittled, doubted, or unworthy. Verbal abuse can also prevent a person from reaching their full potential (if they allow it.)

This form of abuse attacks one's inner ability. Previously we dealt with the ripping apart of a person's exterior. Let us now look at what happens when the interior is attacked.

When we as mothers (or anyone else) convince our daughters they aren't smart enough to get the job, so we tell them to just bat your eyes and get by. This is abuse.

Anyone who saw Suzanne, a 5'7", 24-36-24 beauty, would think she had no problems. But could outward beauty be as big of a hindrance as outward flaws? Yes. If verbal abuse raises its ugly head, the outcome would be the same — a damaged, self-image.

Suzanne was always a beautiful child. Weight was never a problem with her. She took care of her clothes and everywhere she went, even as a child, she turned heads.

Suzanne's sister didn't seem to turn heads, as Suzanne had done. Her sister wore glasses, was overweight for her age and was dark in complexion. While her sister endured her own form of verbal abuse, Suzanne was also verbally abused. But this form was subtle and happening, unaware to Suzanne, her mother or sister. This form is overlooked, because it is hidden in a collection of positive statements.

Suzanne learned to love the compliments and positive looks by guys. She admired herself in the mirror daily, believing what everyone had said of her — that she truly was the fairest of them all.

But Suzanne had a secret. She wasn't smart. She was told it was all right … "No one expects you to be a genius. One day, you will get married and live happily ever after."

Suzanne was sent to art school and her fat sister was sent to a more academic school. Suzanne and her sister were close, despite the outside forces that tried to divide them. Suzanne didn't always like being noticed only for her looks, even though she - like Sherry - had bought into the words that was spoken to her mental "it".

(Read *'Cause I'm a Woman*). Suzanne had ideals and dreams of the corporate world, but because she had not really accomplished much at school, she felt blessed just to make it out of high school.

She fell for the "You're so beautiful" line so much that she became a teenage mother. Her life spiraled downward from there. She continued her promiscuous behavior, which resulted in more pregnancies.

Suzanne, too, had been the victim of verbal abuse and suffered the results thereof.

She had not been encouraged to work hard and use her mind; she was told to "flaunt it and it will be given to you". (On the other hand, her sister was told to "Work hard, because you are too fat and ugly to marry."

No one told Suzanne of the consequences of batting your eyes. She wasn't warned of the emptiness she would feel inside, even after a dozen sexual partners. She had no idea what to do after her looks began to fail and with no education on which to rely.

At 26 years old, Suzanne had a 10-year-old and was unable

to help him with his grammar homework. She felt awful about herself and was looking for a change. She found out that makeup couldn't cover up inner wounds.

Through counseling, she began to deal with some of the words and phrases released from her mother's tongue — phrases like, "You don't have to be smart. You are so pretty, someone will marry you right up," or "You don't need college just get a husband."

Suzanne now knows that her true potential was never tapped into, let alone met.

She was just as abused as was her sister. By not believing she could be both pretty and smart, Suzanne faced a different type of abuse, but abuse nevertheless. She was hindered from fulfilment by the teaching to depend on a man to fulfill her dreams and not to complete college because she was so pretty.

What would have happened if her mother's tongue had appreciated her daughter's beauty but encouraged her not to rest on her loins because of such beauty? What if she had told Suzanne, as she told her other sister, "Study hard. Do your best. You may never get married"?

Think about some of the situation comedy's you have seen on

television. Several of them include a smart, dorky girl and a beautiful, dumb sister. As I reflect on some of the old shows, I think of *Blossom, Three's Company, Eight is Enough, The Brady Bunch, Family Matters,* to name a few. Each of these shows had an acceptable dingle brain whom no one expected to do better.

As mothers, we should always expect and encourage the best from all of our children, regardless of their outward appearances, physical abilities, and/or intellect. Our words should be words of encouragement They should be edifying, wholesome, positive, and full of faith in our children's abilities to subdue, conquer, and have dominion over everything that God intends for them.

Suzanne suffered from her mother's faithless tongue concerning her child's ability. We should never make our children feel as if we doubt or disbelieve in their self worth.

Our goals as parents should be to empower them and not chip away at their self-worth.

Suzanne finished counseling and college. She became successful in her dream job.

Ironically, Suzanne sought acceptance for her mind, as others sought acceptance for their appearances or sizes.

Let's think back to my earlier statement that children just want our acceptance. No strings attached, just pure uncompromising acceptance.

Mother, what words will you release onto your children? Will they be words of life or death? Will the words lift up or tear down? Will the words edify or destroy? What will the next set of words you release onto your children do to them?

Watch that tongue.

Healing starts

When faith reaches out for it,

Grabs hold of it,

Holds onto it,

And walks through it.

Chapter Eight

Blake

Some words cause fear and confusion. These words released onto the child by the parent(s), as a form of control over them, leave the child with the inability to make a decision.

You may find the child second-guessing every decision he makes until his parent(s) are pleased with the final decision.

Blake, 25 and still afraid of making decisions, finds he is always soliciting the opinions of his parents and friends. He is constantly changing his mind if someone doesn't agree with him.

As a five-year-old Blake asked, "Mommy may I have a pop?"

"Yes, you may. Would you like grape or orange?"

"Grape."

"Why don't you get the orange? It won't stain if you spill it on   your clothes."

"I want grape."

"C'mon, drink the orange for mommy. You'll like it."

I see this form of manipulation daily, and I am sure you have seen or been apart of it, as well.

Our children need to learn how to make decisions. Once they have, we do not need to use words, voice tones, or facial expressions to undermine their decisions. Undermining them in such a fashion causes them to fear making decisions altogether.

Several times, I've heard parents in fast food restaurants ask their children what they wanted to eat.

The child would say, "I want chicken nuggets."

"No, you want a hamburger."

Then the war would begin and the parent would buy what they wanted the child to eat. And, of course, the child's lip would go out.

There you have it: the seed of resentment. Why ask your children if you have already made your decision for them? Just give them what you have decided on, and don't start an unnecessary war with your children.

My children once asked me that same question. "Mom, why do you ask us if you have already made the decision?"

Now I don't ask them things I have already made a decision about. If I ask their opinions, I intend to value them, as well.

Sometimes we cause discord in our homes by the way we speak to and treat our children.

Blake was stripped of his decision-making mechanisms, because every decision was challenged and then overturned. He found it easier just to say, "I was thinking about such-n-such. What do you think?" Once he heard his mother's idea, he quickly adopted it as his own.

"That's a beautiful outfit, Blake. But I would have worn the black shirt, instead."

Blake of course began to think something is wrong with the shirt he had on. He eventually changed into the expected behavior.

Why is this mother's tongue so negative? Because she is controlling. Anytime we release words in order to gain control over another human being, we are practicing verbal abuse.

Words are for comforting, edifying, and correcting in a positive manner. Not for manipulation and or the controlling of others.

It is vital for our children to learn to make decisions, and to feel confident — not insecure — in their decisions. Will they always make the right decision? No, of course not. That is where our arms and God's grace come in.

These are the times when we should release comforting words. Words that support and encourage. If we mothers are constantly overturning our children's decisions, demanding they do it our way, they will grow to despise us and be unable to make any decisions.

I know grown men and women who can't make decisions to save their lives. They are forever needing advice and/or help from others. The number one reason for this? Fear. Fear of making the wrong decision keeps them dependent upon others to make decisions for them.

I've been told several times that I have a lot of faith because I move on things others pray about for years. I am convinced some people never get to the heights God intended for them because of fear of deciding. I tell myself, my children, and my class, "If you are not sure about what decision to make, pray and walk in what you hear God say. If you are unsure if you heard God right, move anyway, praying to God that you are moving by faith. And what the devil meant for evil, use it for your glory."

Controlling words breed fear. Isn't this just the behavior Blake's mother was trying to breed?

What we mother sometime forget is that we are raising our children to release them. They won't always be home with us, so we should not cripple them with our unhealthy tongues. *Any words released from our tongues that cause retardation in our children's mind, soul, or body is verbal abuse.*

Our words should motivate, push forward, encourage, correct, and edify. Our words should *always* be delivered in a mild, gentle, or firm tone covered with love. Regardless of what we have to tell our children, when it has all been said and done, our children must know we love them.

Blake's parents did not affirm their love for him. Blake felt he could do nothing right; every decision he made was wrong. His

Father didn't say much, but his mother let him know daily what to think, wear, say and do.

Blake's thinking skills were damaged. His mother created an environment where he didn't need to think.

Blake learned early to conform and keep the peace. In high school, he was a pushover; any sign of disagreement to one of his decisions and he buckled. He had no confidence in his ability to think and make good decisions. He always feared that his choices were dumb ones. His college, and career choice were made for him. Of course, he made his request known. And, of course, it was the wrong one.

This form of verbal abuse is very subtle. You see, this mother loves her son very much and thinks she is doing him a favor by offering her suggestions. She is not telling him what to do; she merely strongly suggests what she would do. Her facial expressions indicated her disapproval until her choice was finally accepted.

She might not even realize that she crippled his decisionmaking process for life.

Now Blake finds himself at work and ridiculed by coworkers.

"Why can't you ever make a decision?"

"Make up your own mind, man."

"How do you ever expect to get ahead if you can't make a decision?"

"Blake, you have some excellent ideas. What are you afraid of?"

These are just some of the remarks Blake would receive from fellow workers. He knew something was wrong, as well. *Why am I always second-guessing myself*, he wondered. *It is true. I do have some good ideas. What am I so afraid of?*

Blake realized that, as a child, every decision he made was the wrong one. So, he shut down that part of his brain and allowed "whomsoever will" to make the decisions for him. But as a young man, he knew he needed to revive that area of his life if he was to live and survive as an adult.

God never intended for us to be controlled by anyone, including our parents. We are commissioned to obey and honor our parents but not to shut down our brains and become robots.

As parents, we must remember our children aren't robots with off and on switches. They aren't mini-adults. They are children with raw, tender, and delicate feelings. They want to express themselves without ridicule.

God felt he could trust me, so He opened my womb twice and blessed me with two sons. I must now prove myself worthy of God's favor and trust by the way that I treat these young men.

A mother's tongue is a powerful tool. It can cause a great deal of hurt, pain, conflict and emotional damage.

On the other hand, that same mother's tongue if governed and under subjection of God's word, can do a great deal of good. It can lift a hung down head. It can turn a frown into a smile. It can make an unbeliever believe.

The tongue weighs just ounces, but it has within it the power to cause life or death.

What about your tongue, Momma? Will you speak life or death to your children?

When they leave your home, will they leave as confident, self-assured positive decision-makers, or beaten, fearful insecure adults?

Because of the grace of God, it doesn't matter where we find ourselves on the totem pole of life. We can always start over. If your tongue has not been used in a proper way toward your children and you know that you have caused damaged to your children, ask for God's forgiveness. Ask your children to forgive you. Don't continue as if nothing ever happened. Acknowledge that you hurt them, and ask for their forgiveness.

Sometimes when we hurt children, if we act as if the damage never happened, we perpetuate the hurt. We give that child yet another emotional blow by acting as if they are making it all up.

Don't do this to your children. Acknowledge your wrongdoing. Explain to your child that you had no idea that you were hurting them so deeply. Then make a family pact that you will not allow verbal abuse to pass onto the next generation of children.

Stand up as a family and vow to stomp out verbal abuse. Encourage children to speak out if something is said that attacks their personhood. Don't get defensive if your children tell you that your words hurt them.

I'm not claiming the child is right. I understand that they are looking from a child's perspective.

Take a breather. Pray. And walk in truth.

Once my sons (Yes, both of them, told me, "We love you, Mom, but we don't like it when you holler at us. When you holler at us, it makes us feel little, and hurt, and sad. (I give them the freedom to tell me when I say anything that attacks their personhood. What I said to them may have been valid, but I did not have to holler at them to get it across.)

Just about every person I know shuts down when they are hollered at. What makes us think our children are any different?

Remember that you are raising your children to release them. What will you be releasing into our society? We have too many horror stories of verbally damaged individuals released into our society — and the results of such abuse, as well.

I do not claim that others aren't out there, but 1-800-ABUSE is the only organization that acknowledged verbal abuse as a form of abuse a few years ago when I would call them nightly. Now God is using me to expose this abuse even more.

Words that are released from our mouths that kill, tear down, cripple, and belittle are abusive. Don't use them.

Do something more positive with your tongue. Release words that breed life.

Though a tiny vessel,

the mighty tongue can release a monumental blow.

Such a blow can knock you down if it is negative,

or

lift you up if it is positive.

Sticks and stones

may break my bones,

but words hurt

a lot worse.

The pain of negative words

destroys generation after generation

after generation….

But the power

of positive words

produces life

generation after generation

It may have happened

to you,

but

you don't have to

make it happen

to the next generation.

Break the cycle.

Speak life.

Just one word

from you

can turn

a frown

upside down.

Stop the hurt.

Start the healing.

Speak life.

One person can make the difference.

Be that one person

Dare to be different.

Dare to be kinder.

Dare to be nicer.

Dare to be love.

Dare to be!

Start a new family tradition.

Speak life.

Speak health.

Speak positive.

Speak healing.

Give the children a reason to smile.

Say something nice.

Family Project Number One:

How many times can you make your children smile today?

Be a positive

Parent.

God trusts you to do the right thing.

Pray for His guidance,

and do the right thing.

Enjoy your children.

They want to enjoy you.

Have fun with each other.

They will be gone
before you know it.

Chapter Nine

On a Positive Note

Thus far, we have covered the results of a negative mother's tongue. Now let us flip the coin and hear of the results from a positive mother's tongue.

In the classroom, I notice that when I release positive words onto the children, heads are lifted, smiles are brighter, and work seems to improve. With my own children, I notice a will to work harder and do more when words of appreciation are released instead of words of failure.

We all like to be appreciated. I like giving flowers while the recipient is still capable of smelling them. I don't believe in waiting until people die before I attempt to express what they mean to me.

Our church recently started a new Bible series, "Interactive Bible Study". In our group, everyone was given a job. I was given the position of "Encourager". (The pastor read the descriptive duties for the encourager, and one member at our team said, "Yeah, that's you.")

I love encouraging people to lift up their heads and go. Go in Jesus. Go in His grace. Go in His love. Go in His peace. But get up and go.

The next two chapters will tell of the wonder of a positive tongue and how awesome it feels to release words of life.

Over the next seven days, fast negativity and complaining. Make a decision to be like Christ, even in your speech.

Give God the next seven days to free you from a negative tongue as He rebuilds your life and others around you with positivity.

Chapter Ten

Rita

Rita, a typical sixteen-year-old girl, has had the pleasure of growing up with a positive tongue speaking over her life. Rita didn't walk on water; she made mistakes like any other teenagers. But what made her different was the way her mother responded to those mistakes. (As we adults compare ourselves to God's word, and then to the life we are living, we should have enough grace from those two views to pour onto our children.)

Rita can only wonder what it feels like not to be loved. She has only heard how she was planned and desired by her parents. They have always encouraged her to do her very best. Sometimes that best would breathe an "A" in math and a "C" in English, but never once did it breath discord and disapproval in Rita.

Her parents constantly looked at the entire picture of their daughter's life and not just one aspect. They understood that she was a child still in the developmental phase and they were the grown-ups. So, they were always mindful of her spirit, never wanting to damage her self-worth.

Have they had to deal with tough issues with Rita? Of course! What parent doesn't? But the way they dealt with problems makes all the difference in the world.

When David was caught in adultery, God called him on it, dealt with it, punished him for it, and was done with it. We, on the other hand, want to deal with our children's sins, punish them and then bring it up for the rest of their lives.

I learned that from my son. He had four semesters of free money for school (one of the semesters provided through my money), yet he did not appreciate the blessing God had bestowed on him. Now he has to pay for school on his own, and he has a much better understanding of the value of a dollar. Yet, he does not like me to bring the failure up.

He states "I know I failed, Mom. But every time you bring it up, I feel like a failure all over again."

Maybe this is why God throws our failures(sins) into the sea of forgetfulness, He doesn't want us rehashing those same feelings over and over.

Perhaps we parents try to get our children to remember so that they don't make the same mistake. But, as they remember the mistakes, they remember the feelings that flowed from such mistakes — hopelessness, failure, disappointing themselves and family. They then can't enjoy the joy of a second chance.

May we all learn to deal with negative situations when they happen. Do as God does; forgive them and throw them away, never to bring up the situation again. We are called to be edifiers, to lift each other up, to encourage one another.

Most of us are hard enough on ourselves, our children included. We don't need another person harping on us.

As parents let us make our home environment a safe haven. Let it be safe - physically, emotionally, and spiritually. Realize that a thirteen-year-old is not a miniature adult but an impressionable child with very sensitive emotions. We can't just release any words over our children and think those words aren't going to have some sort of effect in the child's life.

Rita had wonderful phrases and words released onto and into her. And those words rang loud in her ear as she was about to make major life-changing decisions – on matters such as smoking, sex, stealing, self-worth, and God. Because of her positive environment, Rita made positive choices and lives a positive life.

Words have power! They do what you release them to do.

Rita was told, "You are a blessing. You are wonderful. God loves you and blessed our lives with you. You are no accident; we prayed and God gave us you! As long as you walk with and trust God, there is nothing you can't accomplish."

Rita heard those words from her mother's womb and throughout her life. As she got older it was to no one's surprise that she was the captain of, or leader of, or the first choice of everything on which she placed her hand.

She was told she was a success. She believed she was a success. Therefore, she was a success.

Rita lived out what was spoken over her just as Leroy, Sherry, Suzanne, and Blake lived out what was spoken over them.

Words have power! They do what you release them to do!

What are you releasing into your children, nieces, nephews, cousins, or your own lives by the words of your mouth? What are you living and believing because of the words of another?

Why?

Are you ready to be free?

Chapter Eleven

Michael

This will be short and direct. Michael's mother's mouth (like Rita's mother's words) spoke correct, positive things to their children. Michael's mom made him feel like he could accomplish anything.

She was identical to Rita's mom. She loved Michael, and he knew it by her actions and her speech. Yet Michael's outcome was not as positive as Rita's. He seemed to struggle to believe a bit more than Rita did.

Why? The answer lies in the other tongues around Michael. Michael had jealous, unhealthy tongues around him. Those tongues belonged to relatives, classmates, and church members, and yes, friends. Those tongues did not like the way Michael would hold his head up, so they continuously sent out negative words in an effort for Michael to believe a lie.

There is a segment of children that, no matter what their parents tell them, another voice will carry more weight. I don't know why that is. I am not a psychologist. However, I did learn through psychology classes that some children are just more needy and persuadable than others. No matter what the parents say, these children are easily led by someone else's tongue. They believe you are acting out of love only and are not telling the truth about them.

What do you do as a parent? What would you do if you knew a pedafile lived across the street from you? What would you do if you knew someone kept a loaded gun under a mattress? What would you do if you knew a child who liked to play with matches? What would you do if you walked in and saw a relative beating your child with a bat?

What would you do?

In every situation, I can safely say that you would never allow your child in some of the homes with such situations. And you would run to your child's defense in every situation.

So, what makes verbal abuse so different. I'll tell you. We don't want to step on toes. So, we allow the abuse to occur. Then we go home tour own children and say, "Honey, you have to ignore Uncle Marty. He doesn't know any better."

The damage has been done. The words are released and are now bouncing around in your child's mind, becoming a part of the child's make-up. Is it normal for a mother to walk in, catch someone sexually abusing her child, and then leave the room. Then, when the act is over, take the child home and explain to the child that the adult just didn't know any better? Is that normal behavior?

Why do we allow that same thing to happen to our children's spirits? We allow some unhealthy "it "(read *Cause I'm a Woman*) to brutally attack our children's spirit and self- worth and think nothing of it. I say, step on some toes, crush the whole foot if you must, but protect the child!

Why would you allow all of your hard work to go up in smoke by allowing one unhealthy person to degrade your child? Don't wait until you get home; be your child's advocate right then and there. If you don't feel comfortable speaking to the negative person, then just start defusing the words of the person right there with your child present.

Act like superman blocking bullets. Block each lie with the truth right in front of the abuser. Send him the "Not my child" message.

I would explain to my children right in front of the person that the abuser is the one with the problem. He hates himself; therefore he attacks everyone else. I have told my sons in front of their abusers, "The person talking like that is unhealthy. He deson't like himself, so he puts everyone else down." I then went on to tell them, "But you are who God says you are. You can do everything God says you can do, and you can be everything you believe in your heart you can be."

I am no chicken, and am by no means afraid of fighting.

I was raised in The Robert Taylor's Housing Project, so fighting comes very easy for me. What I had to learn was to put down my weapons and pick up God's. I think I am doing a good job of it, I think.

Show me in the Bible where God just allowed anyone to attack His children without a fight. If anything like that did happen, God gave His permission, and He was doing work on the receiver of the abuse, as in the case of Job. David, and Joseph.

Think about this: you do everything right as a parent. Then at one family Christmas party, you allow all of your hard work to be washed away by one unhealthy family member.

Maybe it is about time someone put him in his place. Why not now? Why not you?

The goal is to protect the child, not to make excuses for or protect the adult.

Give the adult a copy of this book, because somewhere he himself has been damaged. Maybe having him read this book will help him to see himself and desire change.

Pray for people who practice verbal abuse. Protect your children from verbal abusers, as you would any other type of abuser. Protect them right on the spot. Let your children know you are their number one advocate.

When the abuser would say things about the boys, I would

always defuse the words, and then say something to the abuser. We defuse verbal abuse with the word of God. It is funny watching a word abuser squirm for something to say when you hit him with the Word of God. *Nothing* is as powerful as the word of God. Use it daily and protect your children from all forms of abuse.

Michael's mother didn't do that. Being the sweetie that she is, she didn't want to rock the boat or step on toes. So she allowed abusive words to be released; they festered for hours until she got home. Only in later years did she realize that it was too late to defuse them. The damage had already been done.

I believe I read in one of Dr. James Dobson's books that you should discipline a child right away. Don't wait for hours, because they won't remember why you are spanking them.

Words go to work as soon as they are released. So waiting even one hour to attack negativity is too long.

If you think I am exaggerating, stop for a moment and think of some words that were released over you ... words that went un-defused and later an attempt was made to defuse them. Now, which set of words did you believe the most and the longest: the original undefused words, or the attempt to later refute them? Do you still believe them, or did the defusing work? I would love to know. Please email me your answers.

A little leaven leavens the whole lump. Get the sin from amongst you. Protect the child. One very negative person would say when the boys were younger, that defending them the way I did was going to make them "Momma's Boys".

I said, "Well, I'm Momma, and these are my boys. So let it be written; so let it be done."

That guy really wanted to attack my children verbally while I sat silent and listened. Well, not in this lifetime! I can't speak for all parents, but this single mom has invested too much, sacrificed too much, and loves too dearly to allow some unhealthy being to come along and have his way with my boys verbally.

As a nation, we must consider verbal abuse alongside all other forms of abuse. Verbal abuse is just as damaging as the rest. Why it is tolerated is very disappointing to me.

Before living in an Orlando shelter, I tried to get into a shelter in Fort Walton Beach. The lady told me point blank, that just because she could not see any outward signs of abuse, I could not be admitted into the shelter for protection.

She literally turned me away, because she could not see the signs of abuse. The signs were there. Americans are just not trained to see them.

Sometimes we see them much too late. This happened to Michael, a teenager struggling with everything because words were released onto him and left un-defused … or the attempt to defuse the words was made after the damaged had been done.

Is it too late for Michael? Of course not. As long as there is a God, it is not too late for any of us.

I have enjoyed this chapter, because I strongly believe in standing up and fighting for our children. So many problems we adults facewould have been non-existent or minimized if we had an advocate fighting on our behalf.

The children, your children, my children, our nieces and nephews, are the future. The kind of future we have will strongly depends upon the kind of words we release into our children's spirits.

Fight for the children. They are worth it. Defuse verbal abuse in your family.

May we knock it out altogether, one family at a time.

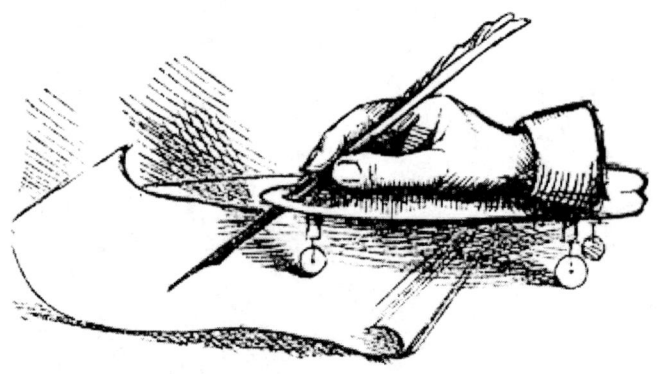

Chapter Twelve

The Son's Tongues

O.J. and Chris Speak

Chris

The truth according to me is amazing, you see, the way something your momma says can change the way you see things.

Yet they swear you don't listen,

and in truth you might be zoned out.

But you can repeat the whole conversation

you two had with no doubt.

And yeah, you make mistakes, and yeah, you make them mad,

but it seems with their words,

they can only make you sad,

or angry anyway,

so you try to get away,

but alas you ain't legal,

you have no choice but to stay.

So you seclude yourself

as best you can,

and wait until the day

you are legally a man.

You lost her trust a long time ago,

so you don't care anymore,

and you no longer partake

in those childish verbal wars.

She calls your cell ten times,

you're just going to the store.

When you're out, having fun

"What she want me home for?"

"I'm not doing nothing wrong,

got nothing to do at home,

Can't I just be left alone?",

"I can't wait 'till I get grown,

so I don't have to deal with this,

I just want to chill, and I know

I'm going to make it,

because I got that skill.

But with all of these things combined,

you still love her,

you don't have a choice

after all, she's your mother.

Like no other, who always told you

you could do it?

Even though she also always told you

that you probably wouldn't.

Also, who always told you

she loved you no matter what?

Even though when she was mad,

she would yell at you like a mutt.

"Cut it out, stop thinking

about the negative mother.

What's wrong with leaving you home

so I can chill with my brother?"

Hey, a mother's tongue can

be confusing at times,

because it heals your wounds,

while prosecuting your crimes.

It can snap like a whip,

and cut like a razor,

but all in all,

it's a behavior appraiser.

It tells you what you're doing wrong,

tries to tell you what is right.

At the same time it's slapping you,

it's telling you to fight.

It knows you're gonna do

what you're gonna do,

even if just out of spite.

And it knows sometimes

you'll have it up all night.

So the best it can do is

warn you, and warn you,

and when you get busted,

it tells you it warned you.

And now you think it scorns you,

but really its just love.

Angry love nevertheless is still love,

It's the best.

You think that you

want all the rest,

but go ahead, stick out your chest

and do your dirty.

I bet you will regret it

'til you're thirty.

So don't be trying to run away

all in a hurry.

Sit back, relax, let mom

buy your McFlurry.

Otherwise you'll be broke,

and probably resort to crime.

And I will tell you right now

don't sweat none of those "dimes".

Girls will come, and girls will go,

but you won't go anywhere

if they are all you care for.

Trust me, don't even think

about these girls

'til you get older,

or you'll end up

with more "ex" files

than Scully and Mulder.

Trust me, I've been there,

It's not what you want to do.

Keep yourself tight in school,

at least just make it through.

By the way, these are things

your mother will tell you. too,

but you're bound not to listen,

you'll just do what you do.

And when your girl gets pregnant,

and you don't graduate,

don't blame it on your mom,

she warned you in the first place.

So when she gets mad, and yells,

understand It's still love.

Even though you feel

like hitting her with a brick glove,

just listen up,

and calm down.

Take a trip

into town,

take awhile to chill out.

Play some music,

get down.

Now you go back to the house,

and go straight to your room.

You hear your mother in her room

playing her favorite tune.

Go clean the kitchen, living room

do something nice,

'cause even though your mother's tongue

seems cold as ice,

she really means well, so you might

as well return the favor.

Even if it's not that way,

give life some flavor,

and do something nice

for a change, it won't hurt you.

Then go to bed soon,

'cause your mother

will squirt you with some water

in the morning so you won't be late.

She's just making sure that

in the future you don't hate

your life because

you only got a GED,

and now the only job you can get

is at Mickey D's.

See, no matter how bad

she might seem right now,

in the long run,

your mother isn't holding you down.

A mother's tongue speaks from hurt,

and love, and anger, and joy.

It's not something anyone can play with,

it's not a toy.

It goes off even more

when talking about one of her boys.

Whether good, or bad,

making you glad, or annoyed,

it is what it is,

and it should be enjoyed,

so make the best of it all through your childhood, don't rest on

it. Listen, or you might end up missing, or missing something. At

least think about it later after your mind is done jumping from

subject to subject because you're so zoned out.

                                                                    Chris

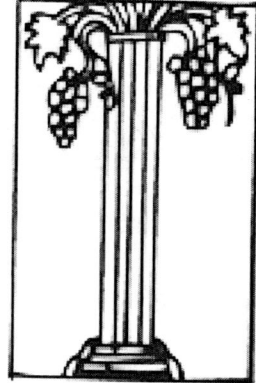

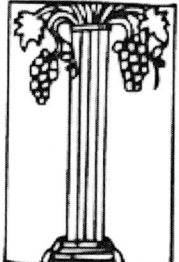

O.J.

When my mom asked me to write this for her book, I was reluctant to ever start. I am very withdrawn about my personal feelings, though you'd be easily deceived by my explosively outgoing personality. Furthermore, it's rare I'll ever expose myself in a way where I express my full, honest position on my own life to anyone. And here I am, writing to the world.

I hope I can tell you something useful. I hope I can give you something to make your existence more fulfilling. I aspire to present you a better understanding of your life. But, frankly, I will not try to.

My mother's tongue was not the only tongue that influenced me. But of all human beings, it was (and is) by far the most influential. It was she who taught me what self-esteem means and how to choose good friends. It was she who taught me to be careful in whom I trusted and to make my own decisions.

Most importantly, she taught me to trust in God. I learned to be a Christian and not a church-goer. She never forced Christianity on me but was diligent to make sure we read the Bible as a family and prayed together. Her words remain important guiding points for my whole life.

Two of the most valuable things she taught me are: to think and to continue thinking differently. I appreciate my ability to reason and to use common sense. Mom's lesson constantly challenged Chris and me to bring our thinking level high enough to make educated decisions on our own. When we asked her questions, she would often respond, "What do you think?" Likewise, when we wanted to know what something meant, she would have us look it up in the dictionary. This way, not only would we know what the word meant; we'd be better equipped to use it correctly.

Obviously my brother and I became more efficient learners, decision makers, and reasoning thinkers. She didn't stop there, though. Our mom never let us believe that we'd find the right answers following "the crowd". Instead, we learned to always deduce for ourselves to which way to go.

To all parents, God revealed to me one day that each child you bring into the world is another chance to change the world. Do your homework. No champion of history was ever perfect. In fact, most preceding heroes were outcasts. Don't think of your child as simply your responsibility; remember that child is your future and the future of the world.

Every day, make valuable contact, encourage your children, and challenge them to think outside of the boundaries of your own life. Don't raise someone to be a good person; raise them to be tomorrow.

One of the most valuable things my mother ever taught me was that she wasn't raising me to be like her; she was raising me to be better. She taught my brother and me that each generation should be better than the last. Understanding was taught through her words, and we knew that we had a responsibility as young men to mature into young adults and to grow into accountable men, husbands, and fathers.

O. J.

Chapter Thirteen

Joe

Yet another form of abuse that is often overlooked. It is the over-achieving parent. This is the opposite of Suzanne's situation, because as no one expected her to achieve.

Everyone expected Joe to succeed. He could bring home nothing lower than a "B"; it was absolutely forbidden for him to bring home any lower grade. Joe was beaten, ridiculed, and verbally assaulted for days when he fell below the expected grade. The entire family was informed of his "B-, or C grade".

Joe felt the pressure to succeed in everything and at all cost. Even if that meant cheating.

I had several experiences with parents and children in this situation. This form of abuse causes children to lie, cheat, and steal in an effort to keep the parent happy and the abuse to a minimum.

One parent said in a conference, "My child is not allowed to bring home anything lower than an 'A'." She then went on to say, "I don't like this grade and I want it changed."

The principle changed it. I kid you not! Even though there were 39 documented grades to justify the "B", the parent didn't like it. So it was changed. (Do you still wonder why there is such a teacher shortage?)

This particular child was only allowed to bring home "A's". One day he received an A- on a test and began to sob so hard and loud that he couldn't breateh. I had to sit him on my lap and release comforting words to him, reminding him of his value outside of that one test. He then stated, "My mom said if I bring home another "A-" I was going to get a spanking."

I had seen the results of some of his spankings. They were not pretty sights. The point is that, no matter what I was speaking into his life at present, that he could only hear his mother's tongue.

This brings us back around to the power of that little instrument. The tongue weighs only ounces but can do tons of damage. Joe was on all counts a good student. He would get mostly "B's". Even though that was the lowest possible grade he was allowed to bring home, even that wasn't enough. There were always the underlying remarks that you could do better, if you can get a "B" you can get an "A".

This is not always true, parents. Allow your children to relax, breathe, and do their very best. The goal is for them to do their best and live up to their potentials.

You be their examples, not their drill sergeants.

The child could not bring home anything lower than an "A" parent flunked out of one college and received a couple of "F's" at another.

One parent falsified records to get her child moved up to a higher grade. Parents have gone crazy placing high demands to succeed on 7 and 8 year olds. And we, as a society, wonder why our children are flipping out by the time they reach high school.

Parents, relax. Nothing really counts on their records until high school.

Yes, work on study habits, reading skills, spelling, etc. But don't put college pressure on an 8-year-old.

Third graders should not be crying because of a 91 percent score. Something is wrong with a situation such as this one. Please don't let me be the only one who thinks so. Email me and let me know if you agree or disagree with me here.

Being a teacher's assistant for 10 years, and then having my own classroom for five years, has enabled me to stumble upon some truths when dealing with children. One is that all children (including mine) lie when their backs are up against the wall. They start around two and just learn to be masters at it as they get older.

The most dangerous parents on earth are parents who really believe that their children don't lie. I have had those parents and those children in my class before, and it is a very sad sight. While the mothers are convinced their children don't lie, the children are sharpening their skills and becoming masters at their craft.

Another tough example is those parents who believe their children tell them everything. They don't. I have had several parents who believe this one.

I recognize children who are under extreme pressure to perform, and therefore always try to have a classroom environment where they can feel free to learn, know that they are loved, and feel free to express themselves. I see them acting out and up, I hear them as they verbalize their feelings towards their parents, and then I see them conform to the expected image when the parent arrives to pick them up.

The goal is to have a school and home environment conducive to learning, loving, and acceptance. Today's teachers are expected to do it all — educate and raise the child, Hopefully, this book will reveal the importance of the home and especially the mother's tongue.

Kids repeat more of their mothers' words than their dads', and for a lot of my little African-American sisters and brothers, our mother's tongue was all we had. So, of course, it carried a lot of weight.

Mothers, hear me. Fathers, hear me Society, hear me. There is another form of abuse that we must recognize as strongly as the others: — verbal abuse. And it is a killer. It kills mentally, spiritually and - at times - physically.

But every one of us has the tools needed to stop this killer. So let us stand together to put an end to this unruly evil.

We are to build up our children with our words and not tear them down. The book of James says that bitter and sweet water should not come out of the same fountain. Before you speak to your child or anyone, ask, "Are the words I am about to release going to lift this person up or tear them down?" Act accordingly.

I am not advocating that we hide or distort the truth with sweeties and honeys. We must remain honest at all times, even if the truth hurts. I am talking about degrading, damaging, and belittling words that cause one to feel less of a person. I am talking about calling a child *stupid* because he or she spilled a cup of milk. Or calling a teenager *sorry* because he can't find his keys. Or calling a boy *scared* because he doesn't want to play football with the gang. Labeling a girl *sluttish* just because she carries herself like she loves herself. Calling a child *backward* because he writes with his left hand. A girl *strange* because she likes cars instead of dolls.

Get the picture?!!! I am talking about any language (verbal, or physical) that causes children to drop their heads in shame.

Chapter Fourteen

Children are a Blessing

I am going to wrap up at this time, because I really want to get this book into your hands. There will definitely be a *Mothers Tongue 2*. It will include your victories, successes and failures. Its purpose will be as this one is: to spread the word of how powerful words are and how we as mothers can change the direction of our children's lives just by the words we release over and into their lives.

I am so looking forward to hearing from you. Please feel free to email me and let me know what this book has meant to you.

Love 'ya. Remember, you are not standing alone. There is help available. Be encouraged, and encourage all within the sound of your voice

Until,

Carolyn Denise

carolyndenisekemp@msn.com

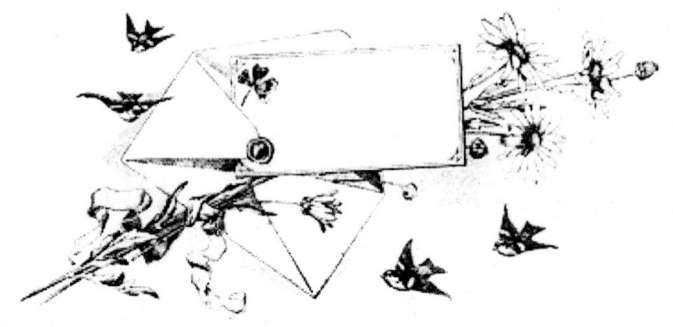